Note to Parents and Teachers

The READING ABOUT: STARTERS series introduces key science vocabulary to young children while encouraging them to discover and understand the world around them. The series works as a set of graded readers in three levels.

LEVEL 2: BEGIN TO READ ALONE follows guidelines set out in the National Curriculum for Year 2 in schools. These books can be read alone or as part of guided or group reading. Each book has three sections:

• Information pages that introduce key words. These key words appear in bold for easy recognition on pages where the related science concepts are explained.
• A lively story that recalls this vocabulary and encourages children to use these words when they talk and write.
• A quiz and index ask children to look back and recall what they have read.

Questions for Further Investigation

FIRE AND ICE explains key concepts about CHANGING MATERIALS. Here are some suggestions for further discussion linked to questions on the information spreads:

p. 5 *Why should you be careful near hot fires or cookers?* Ask children to think about safety issues, e.g. near fires, cookers, kettles, toasters, fireworks, hot food, hot surfaces.

p. 7 *Why shouldn't you play with a ball near windows?* Ask children about other objects that can break easily, e.g. plates, glasses, cups. Also mention dangers of broken glass.

p. 9 *Could a brick be made back into soft clay?* Explain idea that some processes are irreversible, e.g. a cake cannot be made back into dough.

p. 11 *What happens when something is cooked for too long?* Ask children if they can describe what happens when toast burns, e.g. smoke and burnt smell and taste.

p. 13 *What else melts when it gets hot or warm?* e.g. butter on hot toast, snow and ice.

p. 15 *Do you think big lumps of ice melt faster than small lumps?* Small lumps melt faster (due to greater surface area relative to volume). Could ask children to use ice to find the warmest place in a room and to make it a fair test by using lumps that are the same size.

p. 17 *How could you make the frozen bread soft again?* By warming it up – defrosting. Explain idea of reversible processes, such as water turning to ice and back to water.

p. 19 *What happens to cold glass when you blow on it?* Our breath contains water too. When we breathe on cold glass, it steams up. The water in our breath turns into droplets.

p. 21 *Do you know where wool comes from?* Could also ask about leather, silk, coal.

ADVISORY TEAM

Educational Consultant
Andrea Bright – Science Co-ordinator, Trafalgar Junior School, Twickenham

Literacy Consultant
Jackie Holderness – former Senior Lecturer in Primary Education, Westminster Institute, Oxford Brookes University

Series Consultants
Anne Fussell – Early Years Teacher and University Tutor, Westminster Institute, Oxford Brookes University

David Fussell – C.Chem., FRSC

CONTENTS

© Aladdin Books Ltd 2005

Designed and produced by
Aladdin Books Ltd
2/3 Fitzroy Mews
London W1T 6DF

First published in
Great Britain in 2005 by
Franklin Watts
96 Leonard Street
London EC2A 4XD

A catalogue record for this
book is available from the
British Library.

ISBN 0 7496 6247 6

Printed in Malaysia

Editor: Sally Hewitt

Design: Flick, Book Design
and Graphics

Thanks to:
• The pupils of Trafalgar
Infants School, Twickenham for
appearing as models in this book.
• Lynne Thompson for helping
to organise the photoshoots.
• The pupils and teachers of
Trafalgar Junior School,
Twickenham and St. Nicholas
C.E. Infant School, Wallingford,
for testing the sample books.

Photocredits:
*l-left, r-right, b-bottom, t-top,
c-centre, m-middle*
Cover tl, tr & b, 5br, 16tr, 23b, 24tr,
27ml — Comstock. Cover tm, 22,
23tr — Corbis. 2tl, 5br, 16b, 31tr —
European Community. 2ml, 8b, 12b,
14br, 15 both, 17tr, 19tl — PBD. 2bl,
13b, 31br — Rexam plc. 3 — US
Navy. 4, 30ml — Digital Vision. 5tr,
8tr, 8mr, 9 bl, 11tr, 12t, 17bl, 18b,
25 both, 31bm & br — Jim Pipe. 6
both, 9t, 13tl, 21tr — Marc Arundale
/Select Pictures. 7t — Pilkington
Building Products-UK. 7br —
Columbus, GA. 11b — Select
Pictures. 11br, 12tr, 14t, 21bl, 31tl,
32 — Ingram Publishing. 18tr — Flat
Earth. 19br — Flick Smith. 20tr —
David Nance/ USDA. 21b, 26tr,
26ml, 27br, 30tr, 31mr — Photodisc,
24 — Brand X Pictures. 26br — Ken
Hammond /USDA. 27tr, 28b, 29 both
— Bob Nichols/USDA. 28tl — Corel.

READING ABOUT

Starters

CHANGING MATERIALS
Fire and Ice

By Jim Pipe

Aladdin/Watts
London • Sydney

The things in your house are made from different **materials**.

Wood makes tough tables and chairs.
Plastic makes waterproof mugs.
Glass makes transparent windows.
Cloth makes soft clothes.

We **change materials** to make things.
We can cut them or shape them.

Materials also change when they burn. In a fire, wood turns to ash.

We also **change materials** by making them hot or cold.

Making water very cold turns it to **ice**. Making water hot turns it to steam.

A very hot **fire** can make even metal melt!

Ice cream

• Why should you be careful near hot fires or cookers?

You can change materials with pushes and pulls.

You can **stretch, squash** or **twist** a ball of clay.

If you **squash** a plastic ball, it changes shape. Let go, and it changes back!

A woolly hat stretches to fit on your head.

Squashing a ball

6

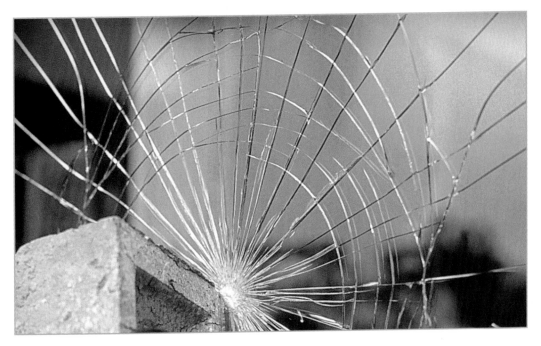

Broken glass

Other materials are hard to **stretch** or **squash**. If we hit glass hard, it breaks.

But if we heat glass or metal, they go soft. Then we can make them into new shapes.

This blacksmith is heating metal so he can bend it.

• Why shouldn't you play with a ball near windows?

Materials change when you **heat** them. When metal in a toaster gets hot, it **glows** red.

When you **heat hard** corn it turns to fluffy popcorn! Guess what sound it makes?

Popcorn

Clay bricks

Heat from the Sun turns soft clay into hard bricks too!

Wet clay is **soft**. It can be squashed into small bricks.

The clay can be **heated** in a hot oven.

The **heat** changes the clay. It becomes a **hard** brick.

• Could a brick be made back into soft clay?

When we heat food, we **cook** it. The heat changes the food.

When we **cook** a runny egg, it goes firm.

We also **cook** dough to make biscuits.

These children are mixing the **ingredients** together to make the soft dough.

Mixing dough

10

Oven

The dough is put into an **oven**.
The hot **oven bakes** the dough.

The soft dough turns
brown and hard.

The **ingredients** have
changed into biscuits.
Yummy!

Biscuits

• What happens when something is cooked for too long?

When some materials get hot, they **melt**. They go soft or **sticky**. They also change shape.

Look how cheese **melts** on a hot pizza.

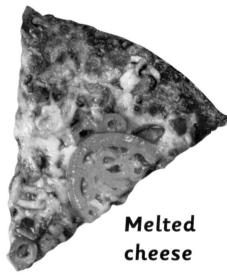

Melted cheese

Chocolate

If you hold chocolate, your warm hands make it **melt**.

It gets very **sticky!**

What happens when it gets **cool** again?

12

When glass is put into a hot fire, it **melts**. Then it can be made into different shapes.

This hot glass is being made into bottles.

A hot flame of a candle melts the wax. Watch out, it can burn you!

• What else melts when it gets hot or warm?

Ice cream cones

Cold **ice** cream is hard. But if you eat an **ice** cream on a hot day, it melts fast.

When the **ice** in **ice** cream melts, it turns to **water**.

The **ice** cream runs down the cone!

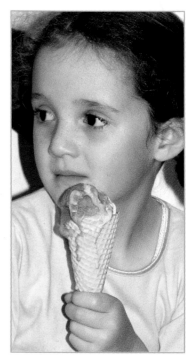

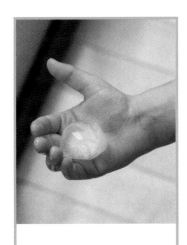

Hold a lump of ice in your hand. Brrrr! It's cold!

Take some **lumps** of **ice** out of the freezer. Put some **lumps** in a warm place. Put other **lumps** in a cold place.

Wait for 30 minutes and take a look.

The **ice** in a warm place will melt faster than **ice** in a cold place.

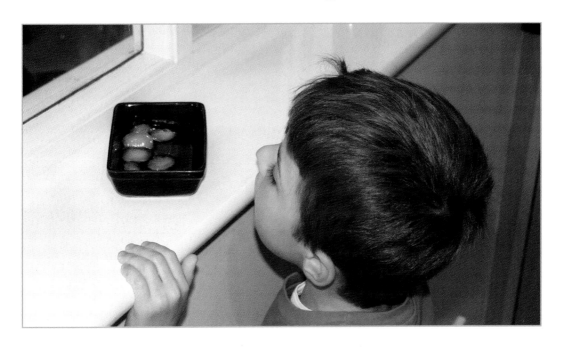

• Do you think big lumps of ice melt faster than small lumps?

Water turns to ice when it gets very cold. It **freezes**. It goes hard like a stone.

In very cold places, even seas and rivers turn to ice.

When it is very cold, rain turns to snow.

Materials with water in them change when they **freeze**.

This girl has put some bread and baked beans into a **freezer**.

Water in the bread turns to ice, so the bread goes hard.

The beans turn rock hard too.

The water in the beans has turned **solid**.

• How could you make the frozen bread soft again?

When water gets very hot, it **boils**. The heat makes it bubble.

When water **boils**, it turns to **steam**. It rises into the air. Be careful! **Steam** is very hot.

Old trains used steam in their engines.

Boiling water

When you run hot water in a bath, it makes **steam** too.

When the hot **steam** touches a cold window, it cools down.

The **steam** turns back into tiny drops of water.

So **steam** and ice are both water!

• What happens to cold glass when you blow on it?

We use heat and forces to change materials into everyday things.

Some materials come from plants and animals. We call them **natural** materials.

Cotton is a natural material. It grows on a bush.

Cotton shirt

Wool socks

Leather boots

Many clothes are made from **natural** materials such as cotton, wool and leather.

20

Natural materials also come from the ground. Stone comes from rocks. Clay is a kind of soil.

Metals come from rocks called **ores**. Big machines dig **ores** from the ground.

• Do you know where wool comes from?

When we change natural materials into useful things, we **manufacture** them.

Bowl

Cutters

Rolling pin

We cut and smooth wood to make a wooden rolling pin.

We heat and squash metal to make forks, spoons and cutters.

We shape china clay then bake it hard to make bowls and plates.

Machines mix natural materials to make new ones. These are **manufactured** materials.

Glass is made from sand. Plastics are made from oil under the ground.

Machines turn wood into the paper in this book.

Glass jars

• What things can you find that have been manufactured?

THE FOREST FIRE

Look out for words about **fire** and **ice**.

Today our class is visiting a forest.

We all **squash** onto the school bus. Mrs Yip and Mr Briggs, our teachers, get on last.

The Sun shines into the bus. It's **boiling** hot! "It's like an **oven** in here!" says Jo. Barry **stretches** over to give her some water. "Thanks! That will **cool** me down," says Jo.

We drive through the town. I sniff the air.
"Mmm, someone's **cooking**," I say.
"It must be that **bakery**," says Anita.
"Look at those cakes!"
"They make me hungry," says Justin.

I look for the chocolate in
my pocket. Oops, it's **melted**.
It's all **soft** and **sticky.**

"Still want a **lump**?"
I ask Justin.
"No thanks!" he laughs.

Later, we drive
past a factory.
Steam pours from
the chimneys.

"That factory uses wood from the forest to
manufacture paper," says Mrs Yip.

As we get near the
forest, Mr Briggs
points to a cloud of
smoke. "That looks
like a **fire**," he says.

A **fire** engine goes past.
The driver waves at us.

"I think it's safe to
keep going,"
says Mrs Yip.

"Look," says Anita.
"That's where the **fire** was."

I **twist** around. The trees
are black like burnt toast.

We arrive at the park. "Let's
cook lunch!" says Justin.

"We might set the forest on
fire again!" says Mr Briggs.

On our walk we find
a stream. Jo dips her
hand in the water.
"It's **freezing**," she says.

"That water is **melted**
ice and snow from
the mountains,"
says Mrs Yip.

We collect leaves and other **natural materials** for our art project.

Suddenly, there is a very loud noise. A **fire** engine rushes past again.

"Everyone back to the bus!" says Mr Briggs. From the bus, we watch the **fire** fighters.

One of the **fire** fighters walks over.
"Don't worry,"
she says.
"We can soon put
out the **fire.**"

When it is safe,
the bus drives back.

"Look at the smoke," says Brian.

"The **fire** has
also **changed**
some of the
water into
steam," says
Mr Briggs.

Some of the
wood is still
glowing red.

Back at school, we tell
everyone about the **fire**.

"That **fire** was a bit scary,"
says Mrs Yip. "But you were very brave so
Mr Briggs and I will buy
everyone an **ice** cream."

"Eat them quickly
before they **melt!**"

Can you write a list of things that
change when they get hot or cold?
Draw a picture to show what happens.

The cake bakes
in the oven.

The hot Sun
melts the
snowman.

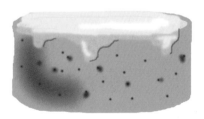

QUIZ

How can we bend **materials** like metal?

Answer on page 7

Why does **ice** cream **melt**?

Answer on page 14

Where do **natural** **materials** come from?

Answer on page 20-21

Can you remember how these materials change when you heat them?

Glass

Water

Egg

Have you read this book? Well done! Do you remember these words? Look back and find out.

INDEX